The Inheritance Book

The Inheritance Book

What you need to know about receiving and investing an inheritance from the U.S. when you live in Israel

Douglas Goldstein, CFP®

With special guest articles on wills and estates by
Russell D. Mayer, Adv.

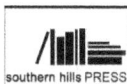

southern hills PRESS

Pittsburgh

Published by Southern Hills Press, Pittsburgh, PA, USA

Cover design by Rehmat Ullah

Interior design by Ayala Cohen-Salmon

ISBN 978-1-933882-17-8 The Inheritance Book (Soft cover)

ISBN 978-1-933882-18-5 The Inheritance Book (Kindle)

Contents

About the author

Douglas Goldstein, CFP®, is the founder and director of Profile Investment Services, Ltd.

Since 1997, Doug's Jerusalem-based company has been helping people living in Israel open and maintain U.S. investment and retirement accounts. Frequently, folks who receive an inheritance, are planning for retirement, or just need help with their stocks, bonds, and mutual funds, call him for assistance.

In 1992, Doug began his career on Wall Street at Dean Witter. After developing a successful practice in New York, he moved with his wife and family to Israel.

Doug is accredited by the Israel Securities Authority (ISA) as a licensed Israeli advisor and is also a licensed

U.S. advisor. He holds the designations of Certified Financial Planner™ in the United States, Registered Investment Advisor, and Trust and Estate Practitioner. He is a member of both the Financial Planning Association and of the Society of Trust and Estate Practitioners.

Doug teaches undergraduate and graduate courses on investing and is often invited to comment on financial affairs on radio, TV, and in local and international newspapers.

In addition, Doug's advice appears in the weekend edition of *The Jerusalem Post*, and he hosts a weekly financial podcast and radio broadcast, *The Goldstein on Gelt Show*, especially designed for Americans living in Israel. He is the author of the books *Building Wealth in Israel: A Guide to International Investments and Financial Planning*, co-author of the best-selling *Rich As A King: How the Wisdom of Chess Can Make You a Grandmaster of Investing*, and several others as well.

Before you start reading

Before you start reading, go to:
www.Profile-Financial.com/inheritance-intro
to watch a brief video message from Doug.

Introduction

❦

If you're dealing with an inheritance from a loved one, or if you'd like to know what will happen to your assets when you're gone, this book is for you. In particular, the following pages will help people living in Israel who are handling an inheritance coming from the United States.

WHAT HAPPENS WHEN AN AMERICAN CITIZEN LIVING IN ISRAEL PASSES AWAY?

Executors and heirs are often left with a number of technical questions:

- What are the mistakes that you, as an heir, should be careful to avoid?

- Can or should you sell the investments that you inherited?

- When do you have to pay inheritance tax (if any), and to which tax authorities?

- How do you claim the inheritance itself, especially if it includes assets in the United States?

WHAT PAPERWORK DO YOU NEED?

When dealing with both the Israeli and American legal systems, these questions become a little harder to answer. If the executors and/or the heirs are not familiar with Hebrew and the Israeli system, the situation may seem even more complicated.

This book provides brief, practical guidelines for managing an inheritance –

- how to deal with probate,

- what happens if there is no will, and

- what to do with the actual inheritance once you receive it.

Don't use this book as the "final word" related to any legal, pension, tax, or investing questions, since it's designed to be general in nature and for educational purposes only. Be sure to speak to a licensed professional before making any investment or legal moves.

BONUS FROM "BUILDING WEALTH IN ISRAEL"

In *The Inheritance Book* you will find a bonus chapter from my book, *Building Wealth in Israel*, which highlights information on the importance of estate planning. As you read, you will find clear explanations detailing how inheritance mistakes and difficulties can be prevented when you originally make a will. Learn if a will or a trust is better in your situation, and decide who can help you make sure that your final wishes will be carried out when the time comes.

FREE RESOURCES

This book provides links to various websites, online tools, and useful checklists that you can download for free. To easily access all this information, we've consolidated the URLs mentioned in this book (and more) on this page: **www.Profile-Financial.com/ inheritancebook.**

Finally, my office in Jerusalem frequently deals with people who have received, or are in the process of getting an inheritance. If you have questions about investing money or handling an inheritance, please contact me.

Douglas Goldstein, CFP®
doug@profile-financial.com
Israel: 02-624-2788
Toll-free from USA: 1-888-327-6179

What Paperwork Do You Need to Claim Your Inheritance?

If you are named as a beneficiary in someone's will, the money doesn't magically appear in your account after the person dies. There are several steps that you need to take in order to receive the assets left to you. Here is a brief guide to those steps, including a listing of the necessary paperwork:

- If the inherited assets and/or property are in Israel, the first step you need to take is to apply to the Inheritance Registrar for a probate order, even if you live abroad, as Israel doesn't recognize foreign court orders. If any of the assets are located in the

United States, you must also file for a probate order in America. However, very often, the United States will accept the Israeli probate order by commencing an ancillary proceeding in a local court in the U.S. This serves to supplement the Israeli court order by having the local court recognize and approve the decision of the Israeli court – the documents required for the process will depend upon the state in which the proceeding is commenced. In any case, you will likely want to hire a lawyer to help you with this procedure. You are not required to use the same lawyer who wrote the original will.

- If you hire a lawyer to do probate for an Israeli will, but you are not located in Israel, you will need to sign a power of attorney either in the Israeli consulate or in the presence of a notary who must have Apostille certification on the document. Apostilles authenticate the seals and signatures that notaries (and other officials) put on important documents. They are used so that courts in one country will accept the validity of a document issued or certified in another country when both countries are party to the applicable international convention.

- When applying for a probate order at the Inheritance Registrar in Israel, the following documents need to be presented:

1. An official application for a probate order. If you are in Israel, this document needs to be signed in the presence of an Israeli lawyer. If you are abroad, it needs to have the certification of the consulate or a notary with Apostille certification.
2. Power of Attorney if your lawyer is making the application on your behalf (same means of witnessing the signing as above).
3. Death certificate.
4. Original will – if signed abroad, often together with an Israeli notarial translation.
5. Signed authorization from your fellow heirs (if there are any) that you are making this application, or an official notice to them sent by registered mail which says that the proceeding is being commenced (enclose a copy of the will).
6. If the deceased lived outside Israel, the legal opinion of an Israeli lawyer with respect to the applicable foreign law regarding the inheritance.

• For brokerage and bank accounts in the United States, you will likely need some of the following documents. Ask each firm where the deceased had an account what will be required:

1. Original Affidavit of Domicile. This completed affidavit will need to be notarized. The brokerage firm or bank will provide you with a blank form. (Go to the free resource page to see a sample of this form.)

2. Consular Report of Death of a U.S. Citizen Abroad. You can obtain this form at the U.S. Consulate. (Go to the free resource page to access this form.) According to the U.S. State Department, a Consular Report of Death of a U.S. Citizen Abroad is:

   - Issued by the U.S. embassy or consulate upon its receipt of the foreign death certificate or finding of death by a local competent authority.

   - An administrative document that provides essential facts about the death, disposition of remains, and custody of the personal estate of the deceased U.S. citizen.

   - Generally used in legal proceedings in the United States as proof of death.

   - Based on the foreign death certificate, and cannot be completed until the foreign death certificate is issued. (This can take as long as four-to-six weeks, depending on the country.)

To obtain an official copy of the *Report of Death*, the deceased's legal representative must provide to the U.S. Consulate:

- DS 2060 form (go to the free resource page to access this document),
- Original local death certificate,
- The deceased's American passport,
- The deceased's Social Security Number,
- A copy of your passport (if you are the next of kin),
- A notice of death by the hospital or a physician, mentioning the cause of death.

After providing this information to the consulate, it should take four to six weeks to get 20 certified copies. Before your initial visit to their office, call them to confirm exactly what they require since they may update this information from time to time, and you don't want to have to go back additional times.

3. Transfer Certificate. The U.S. Treasury (Regulation Section 20.6325-1) states that estates of certain non-resident decedents must obtain a "transfer certificate" prior to the request for transfer of assets from the decedent's accounts. The transfer certificate issued by the IRS generally represents evidence that the decedent's estate has met its U.S. tax liability obligations. A qualified accountant can assist you with this important document. The IRS takes months to issue the transfer certificate, so start on this process as soon as possible. Documents you will need in order to file a request for a transfer certificate include:

- Either (a) State Department Form DS-2060, which is the Report of the Death of an American Citizen, or (b) death certificate and a copy of the photo page of the decedent's current U.S. passport or other proof of U.S. citizenship.

- An affidavit, which is a written declaration made under oath before a notary public or other comparable local official (this is different from the "Affidavit of Domicile" mentioned above). The affidavit may be in the form of a letter. It must be signed by the executor, administrator, or other personal representative of the estate and include (a) a listing of all assets worldwide in which the decedent had any interest at the date of death, together with their values on that date, and (b) all taxable gifts made by the decedent after 1976. For any U.S. bank or investment account, one should include the account number.

○ One copy of each inventory filed with domestic or foreign probate authorities, with English translations if in another language.

○ One copy of each death tax or inheritance tax return and any corrective statements filed with taxing authorities other than the United States, with English translations if in another language. If the decedent's country of residence does not have a death tax or inheritance tax, provide a copy of the decedent's last income tax return, and a copy of any wealth tax return filed.

○ Copies of the decedent's last will and testament along with any codicils, with English translations if in another language.

On the IRS website (see our free resource page for the link to the website) from which the above list comes, they also note, "If any of the above-listed items are not available, include a statement to explain why. The time frame for the IRS to process the affidavit and supporting documents is 90 days from the time the IRS receives all necessary documentation."

As you work on the Transfer Certificate paperwork, it would be wise to organize the following papers as well, in order to help you comply with the IRS requirements:

- List of worldwide assets and their value at the date of death (go to our resource page for a link to an easy-to-use Excel spreadsheet that you can download for free),

- Bank statements as of the date of death and as of current date,

- Brokerage statements as of the date of death and as of current date,

- Value of all real estate as of the date of death,

- Value of all other assets as of the date of death, including pensions, *Keren Hishtalmut*, *Kupot Gemel*, property, etc.,

- Copies of any U.S. gift tax returns from after 1976, if applicable.

If the deceased's estate is worth **over $11.2 million** (as of 2018), the IRS requires you to file:

1. Form 706, which is the United States Estate Tax Return (go to the free resource page to access this form), together with the supporting documents specified in the Form 706 Instructions. The return is due nine months after the decedent's date of death.
2. Either (a) State Department Form DS-2060, which is the Report of the Death of an American Citizen, or (b) death certificate and a copy of the photo page of the decedent's current U.S. passport or other proof of U.S. citizenship.

RECEIVING AN INHERITANCE FROM AN IRA (INDIVIDUAL RETIREMENT ACCOUNT)

- IRAs distribute assets directly to beneficiaries without having to go through probate, so the decedent's will does not matter in dealing with the payouts from IRAs. Instead, the financial firm managing the IRA will provide you with beneficiary forms and will require you to sign a W-9 (for

American citizens) or a W-8BEN (for non-U.S. citizens). (Go to the free resource page to access these forms.) **Before** asking for a distribution, determine if you are allowed to set up a "stretch" or "beneficiary IRA," which could allow you to keep the money in a tax-deferred account for many years to come. Check with your accountant or financial advisor to find out if you could transfer the assets directly into another IRA in your name. Find out more about beneficiary IRAs by listening to *The Goldstein On Gelt Show* episode, "Stretch IRAs – A Great Way to Pay Taxes Later". (Go to the resources page for a link to the episode.)

• Non-U.S. citizens will require an original death certificate for each account, along with an English translation. The original must have a genuine stamp or seal on the document. Order enough extra originals so that you can provide an original to every financial institution where the deceased had an account.

Resource: How to Avoid the Pitfalls of Estate Administration

Efficient estate administration minimizes the amount of time it takes heirs to receive an inheritance. **Estate expert Peggy Atkins Munro**, author of *Estate and Trust Administration for Dummies*, explains the basics that everyone should know when dealing with an estate, whether it is preparing your own estate or an inheritance. Find out the difference between a will and an estate plan and why both are important.

Go to the free resource page at **www.Profile-Financial.com/inheritancebook** to find a link to this interview.

2

What Everybody Ought to Know About Wills

When dealing with an original will prepared by an American citizen, you may need to work with the legal systems both in Israel and the United States. This does not have to be too complicated if you follow the guidelines below. This chapter is designed to summarize some important points. The guest chapter at the end of the book by Russell Mayer, a U.S. and Israeli lawyer, goes more in depth on the concepts.

In the United States, each state has its own probate laws. Therefore, you will have to investigate the legal requirements in the state where the deceased had assets or some legal connection. Ask the advice of a competent estate attorney who has knowledge of inheritance laws in the United States.

If you need to apply for probate in the United States and the original will was written in Hebrew, you will have to obtain an English translation together with Israeli notary certification. Similarly, if the original will was written abroad in English and it refers to assets in Israel, it needs to be translated into Hebrew – and notarized.

Israel currently does not have an inheritance tax (as of 2018). However, the American tax code states that regardless of where the deceased's assets are, U.S. income tax and estate tax (i.e., death tax) may apply. For most Americans, with the new tax reforms under President Trump, the Federal estate tax will not make a difference, since a couple has an exemption for all assets under about $22 million (~$11 million per person).

In most cases, it's better to keep inherited assets that are in retirement accounts, such as 401(k) plans and IRAs, in IRA accounts in the United States, since taking the money out of an IRA and bringing it to Israel can trigger a large tax bill. (For more information about dealing with inherited IRAs, read Chapter 4.)

WHAT HAPPENS IF THERE'S NO WILL?

If your relative passed away without leaving a will, according to Israeli law his or her assets are divided among his or her surviving spouse and children. Usually, the spouse inherits all movable property, including the family car. The spouse also inherits half of any additional assets, the rest of which are divided equally among the children. If there is no will, instead of probate you would apply to the Inheritance Registrar or *Beit Din*, as mentioned above, for a succession order. You would need similar documents except, of course, for the will.

NEED INFORMATION ABOUT THE DECEASED'S PENSION FUNDS AND/OR BANK ACCOUNTS?

If the records of the deceased person's bank accounts and/or pension and insurance policies in Israel are not clear and available, you can obtain this information from the Israeli Finance Ministry's website (go to the free resource page for the link). In the online search engine, you will need to provide your *teudat zehut* (National ID number), as well as that of the deceased, and answer several security questions. You will then receive the name and contact details of the banks and/ or insurance companies where the deceased held any accounts so that you can get more detailed information from them.

Jointly owned bank accounts in the U.S. often have a "right of survivorship" provision so that upon the death of one owner and presentation of a death certificate, title goes to the survivor. The U.S. firms may ask for further documentation, like a transfer certificate (see Chapter One), which could delay getting control of the assets. In Israel, jointly owned property (including bank accounts and apartments) are generally considered to be owned proportionately among the owners and there is no right of survivorship – upon the death of the first owner, that owner's share becomes part of his or her estate subject to probate and will not be released by the bank without a court order. As mentioned above, this could be problematic if, for example, a couple owns an account together and the husband dies intestate (without a will). By law, most often, half of his share would go to his spouse while the other half would be divided amongst his children.

Resource: Do Dual Citizens Need a Separate Will for Each Citizenship?

Should dual citizens have separate wills for assets they own in both countries, or does one will cover their global assets?

Go to the free resource page at **www.Profile-Financial.com/inheritancebook** for a link to a 20-minute interview with **Albert Goodwin, a New York estate planning attorney**, about the importance of Americans in Israel having an Israeli will. Goodwin has experience helping people in New York, Florida, and Israel with estate plans. **He advises that if you live in Israel, you definitely need to have an Israeli will.** There is a great deal of red tape involved in trying to use a U.S. will in Israel, as foreign documents and official translations can complicate matters in court.

3

Received Money? What Should You Do Now?

When you receive an inheritance, you may feel over-whelmed. You may wonder what to do with the money that you just inherited. Should you save or spend it? What is the best way to honor the memory of the deceased? Where should you invest it? How much can you spend, and how much should you save? What about charity?

Avoid making any rash decisions. The best thing is to wait a few months until your emotions settle and you are able to think clearly. Start handling transfer paperwork right away, though, since that process can take a long time.

THE THINGS NOT TO DO WITH AN INHERITANCE

When you get an inheritance, your first question may be, "What should I do now?" But perhaps a better question is, "What *shouldn't* I do now?"

AN EMOTIONAL ROLLERCOASTER

Getting an inheritance arouses many emotions. Sometimes, people get too excited and they spend all the money without thinking about the best uses for it. Others feel uncertain about their ability to manage the wealth they just received. Their fear paralyzes them, preventing them from making good monetary decisions.

WHAT ARE THE MISTAKES TO AVOID?

When you receive an inheritance, try not to let the tangle of emotions interfere with making the right choices. Avoid the following:

IMPULSE SPENDING

While you may have always wanted a luxury car, designer jewelry, or the latest technological gadget, step back and ask yourself if these are really the best uses for your new wealth. Sometimes there is an additional cost to an item beyond its price tag – can you afford the ongoing costs of maintaining the new acquisition?

GET-RICH-QUICK SCHEMES

While it may be prudent to invest some or all of your inheritance, don't get blinded by your desire to make as much money as possible. Many offers of "high returns" that sound too good to be true often are, in fact, too good to be true. Sometimes, preservation of wealth is more important than growth. Consult your financial advisor before making any investment decision, since his or her objectivity and knowledge can alert you to scams and unrealistic expectations.

FEAR AND ANXIETY

Don't be too frightened to take some risks. The problem with conservative investments, such as CDs (certificates of deposit in a bank), is that low interest rates may not beat inflation, so in the long run, your money may lose its real value. When rates of inflation are higher than interest rates, the real value of your money diminishes compared with the original investment's purchasing power. A financial advisor can help

you assess your situation and suggest suitable investments. (For more information about the problems
with low-risk investments, see the resource box at the
end of this chapter.)

WHAT EVERYONE OUGHT TO KNOW ABOUT GETTING AN INHERITANCE

Oftentimes, when a person receives a windfall such
as an inheritance, he suddenly discovers many long-
lost relatives and various "old friends" who crawl out
of the woodwork after years of silence. All of them
come knocking on his door, either asking him for
money "because I am in a desperate situation," or
telling him about an amazing investment opportunity
that is "perfect" for him.

When he tries to say no, they may pressure him with,
"You can't let your poor aunt starve," or "I can't let
such a dear friend pass up this great chance of a lifetime."

This type of unrelenting persistence often spells dis-
aster, but such an outcome is easily preventable. Sim-
ply tell these "friends" and "loving relatives" that you
will run their proposal by your financial advisor. See
how many of them will even stick around to hear the
answer. Hopefully, your advisor will be objective and

knowledgeable and be able to tell you whether the request or proposal is genuine or logical and, even more importantly, whether it fits into the design of your financial plan.

Whenever lending money to friends or relatives, consider what would happen if, despite their best intentions, they couldn't repay. Would you and your financial plan be able to turn the loan into a gift? If not, think twice about lending funds.

There is a difference between gifting money and charitable giving. If you receive a windfall, consider giving some of it to charity. Charity can be considered "positive giving" because, if you do your due diligence about the non-profit organization, the money definitely goes to a good cause. In the United States and in Israel (and in many other countries), you can get a tax benefit from donating to a recognized charity, which makes your donation stretch even farther. In addition, if you plan to make a large gift and want to be sure that the money is used for the charitable cause for which it is intended, you may wish to employ the services of a family office to find out how the organization uses its resources.

(You can learn more about family offices at **www.Profile-Financial.com/family-office.**)

Understand the art of giving to the right causes and you and your fortune can go a long way.

HOW QUICKLY SHOULD YOU INVEST THE MONEY YOU INHERIT?

Though it's usually wise to wait before investing an inheritance, sometimes you must take quick action.

WHEN DO YOU NEED TO ACT QUICKLY?

If you inherited a risky position, you should consider liquidating it. For example, a grandfather who always managed the stock portfolio passes away, leaving large amounts of money invested in a few individual stocks. Unable to live on her own, the grandmother who now owns the stock portfolio needs to move to a nursing facility. What would happen if she waited 12–18 months to deal with the account and then, just before she sold the investments in order to pay her bills, the stock market crashed? While you should act quickly in selling risky investments, there is no need to act quickly in buying other investments. Staying in cash for a few months is fine.

HOW MUCH MONEY DO YOU NEED NOW?

If you inherit a portfolio of stocks, ask yourself if you are in a position to wait (possibly for years) to use the money. A fancy car or an exotic vacation is not an emergency expense. On the other hand, paying for home health care or other medical procedures may very well be a question of life and death and cannot be delayed. Any money needed for the near future, regardless of the type of investment it was in when you inherited it, should be converted to liquid assets such as short-term bank deposits, money market funds, and savings accounts. Even if that means selling Grandpa's stocks, it's the right choice. After all, wealth should first and foremost be used for your family's health and well-being.

HOW TO GET THE MONEY QUICKLY

Depending on the account's structure, you may or may not have easy access to the funds. Even if an account is titled "joint account" or "transfer on death," there may be a drawn-out procedure to follow before the money is fully available. Your investment advisor should be able to walk you through the process. Nonetheless, make sure money is available to each spouse separately so that the widow(er) does not face undue financial pressure caused by bad planning.

DON'T BECOME A VICTIM OF "INHERITANCE LOYALTY SYNDROME"

It is common to feel emotional angst after receiving an inheritance. Heirs may have doubts as to whether they are "allowed" to use the assets as they wish, or whether they somehow have to use them in a way the benefactor would have chosen to use them. There are two ways to approach a sudden influx of money:

- Spend it on things you would never have been able to afford otherwise. The downside of this is the risk of increasing your overall cost of living and finding yourself none the richer. For example, if you choose to upgrade your car, would you be able to afford higher insurance payments, gas, and upkeep in the future?

- Incorporate the assets into your overall financial plan. You could use the inheritance to pay off debt (including your mortgage), fund your emergency account, or increase your savings. Other factors to consider are whether you should use the funds for charitable projects or earmark them for an inheritance for your own children.

SELLING INHERITED ASSETS IS NOT BEING DISLOYAL

Some beneficiaries feel an emotional attachment to the inherited assets that prevents them from making logical decisions. A widow may feel that she is disputing her late husband's judgment by selling stocks he carefully chose years ago.

Yet what was good for your benefactor is not necessarily good for you, as everyone's financial situation is unique. It is important to realize that inherited funds are yours, and proper use of the funds means making them jive with the rest of your financial plan. Your benefactor gave you a legacy to use as you wish.

DID YOU INHERIT SOMEONE ELSE'S BROKER ALONG WITH THE INHERITANCE?

If you receive an inheritance, make sure that you only receive financial assets. Before you inherit someone else's financial advisor, consider the following points:

PUT EVERYTHING UNDER ONE UMBRELLA

Consolidating your assets, including the inheritance, in one brokerage account simplifies financial maintenance. Seeing how all of your assets interrelate gives you the bigger picture, making it easier to monitor overall results. While it is possible to diversify with different accounts, overseeing the relationship between various positions is easier when everything appears on a single statement.

YOUR CURRENT FINANCIAL ADVISOR

If you already have an advisor, he can help you invest your inheritance since he is familiar with your situation and needs. Receiving an inheritance is a good time to update/revise your financial plan. Moreover, understanding your current situation is crucial if you are a U.S. citizen living in Israel. For example, it is potentially problematic if an American citizen inherits Israeli mutual funds because the IRS considers those funds "offshore mutual funds" (a.k.a. "Passive Foreign Investment Corporations" [PFICs]) and taxes them much more harshly than American mutual funds. Make sure your advisor understands cross-border financial issues and invests your money accordingly.

The broker who handled the assets before you inherited them may have had good reasons to advise investing the way he did. However, the investments the deceased chose may not be suitable for you.

Also, consider technical issues: If the deceased's broker is in America and you live in Israel, are his office hours convenient for you? What licenses does he hold? Only American licenses, or Israeli ones, too? Being certified on both sides of the ocean means he could understand your situation better. Moreover, let's say the deceased handled his investments through an insurance agent. If that agent only specializes in insurance products, he may not be able to help you invest the funds in very common asset classes like stocks, bonds, and mutual funds if he isn't *also* licensed as an investment advisor. As such, he might not even suggest those to you. Finally, does the broker know how to maintain the tax-deferred status of an inherited IRA account?

DOES YOUR ADVISOR UNDERSTAND BOTH U.S. AND ISRAELI FINANCE?

If you live in Israel, consider using a financial advisor who is familiar with cross-border financial issues, licensed in both the United States and Israel, and able to help you maintain a U.S. brokerage account. If you aren't aware of the issues affecting a foreign trust or inheritance (including inherited IRAs), contact a financial professional who has the experience and licenses to help you. (Take a look at the video,

"How to Open a U.S. Brokerage Account from Overseas" at **www.Profile-Financial.com/inheritancebook**, or see Appendix B at the end of the book.)

> ### Resource: How to Do the Right Thing When You Get an Inheritance
>
> The first thing to do when you get an inheritance is to resolve that you will not make any rash decisions or changes in your lifestyle without thoroughly understanding what you have just received. This is especially true if these assets are complex investments. Listen to the podcast called **How to Do the Right Thing When You Get an Inheritance** to find out why it is important to get guidance from a qualified financial advisor when you find yourself in this situation.
>
> Go to the free resource page at **www.Profile-Financial.com/inheritancebook** to find a link to this 8-minute podcast, and to read some more helpful articles about a few of the topics discussed in this chapter.

4

What Should You Do with an Inherited IRA?

Sometimes, an inheritance can take the form of an IRA (Individual Retirement Account). If you are living in Israel, this can present a number of questions. Here are some of the most common issues that arise, and suggestions as to how to solve them.

WHAT'S THE BEST WAY TO UPDATE INVESTMENTS IN AN INHERITED IRA?

If you inherit an IRA, you must be aware of the regulations concerning transferring the account to you, the "beneficiary." Apart from the technical requirements for processing the account, however, which a financial advisor should be able to handle, people sometimes feel a moral responsibility to abide by, and thus honor, the financial decision-making of the deceased.

When a client once called me about an inherited IRA, he said, "I would like to sell some of the stocks in the account. Am I legally allowed to do so? And if I do, am I being disloyal to my father's memory by getting rid of what he bought?"

PERSONAL FINANCE IS PERSONAL

This client is far from unusual in the loyalty he feels to his benefactor. Many beneficiaries feel as if they are betraying the person who left them the account if they change anything in it. But that is far from being the case.

When choosing investments, you need to have your *own* goals in mind rather than those of the deceased, which may have been quite different. I told my client, "I'm sure your father wanted the best for you, which is why he made you the beneficiary. Improving the IRA's portfolio by acquiring investments that are more appropriate for your situation isn't being disloyal. It's actually the best way to make the most out of the inheritance."

HOW SHOULD YOU OPTIMIZE THE INVESTMENTS INSIDE AN IRA?

If you sell investments inside an inherited IRA, you don't pay U.S. tax on capital gains (profits). You only pay tax when you withdraw money from the account. This is a huge benefit when compounded over many years. Be aware that generally you shouldn't hold an annuity or other tax-advantaged investments like municipal bonds in an IRA. Furthermore, if you've made *aliya* and decide to transfer the funds out of an IRA to an Israeli investment account, the funds immediately become taxable by the U.S. government and therefore, will no longer receive U.S. tax benefits.

CAN I TRANSFER THE MONEY OUT OF THE IRA?

To maintain the tax-deferred status of an inherited IRA, the money must remain in a specially titled account. As an heir, you can transfer the IRA into a "beneficiary IRA" (a.k.a. "stretch IRA") and thus not pay taxes on the account's capital growth and income until money is withdrawn. Transferring the money abroad can jeopardize the tax beneficial status. As many overseas bankers and investment advisors may not know this crucial piece of information, work

33

with professionals who are well-versed in cross-border investing and tax law.

CAN I OPEN A BENEFICIARY IRA FROM ISRAEL?

Many Americans living outside the United States find that U.S. brokerage firms are not willing to set up an account for them, due to restrictions imposed by strict anti-money-laundering legislation. But this does not apply to all companies.

Besides keeping the American tax-deferred status of your inheritance, there are many advantages to having an American brokerage account. For example, U.S. markets are among the most efficient and investor-friendly in the world. You can also diversify easily through the various investment vehicles that a U.S. brokerage account offers, and having this type of account makes U.S. tax reporting a lot easier. If you live in Israel, and have, or want to have, or are inheriting a U.S. investment, bank, or retirement account, you may want to use the "Toolkit for Opening U.S. Brokerage Accounts from Overseas." (You can find the link to the toolkit on the free resource page.)

WHAT ABOUT ESTATE TAX?

Federal taxes do not have to be paid on estates left by U.S. citizens to their American-citizen children, as long as they don't exceed the "federal estate tax exemption," which is $11.2 million per person. As explained in Forbes (find the links to the next two articles on the free resource page):

"[An] individual can shelter $11.2 million in assets from [estate] taxes. Another federal estate law provision called portability lets couples who do proper planning double that exemption. So, a couple could exclude $22.4 million for 2018. Watch out: The law's sunset means that, absent further Congressional action, the exemption amount would revert to the $5 million base [in 2025], indexed."

In a different article, Forbes also reminded readers that even if they don't have to pay federal estate tax, they might be subject to state estate tax: "[If] you live in one of the 18 states or the District of Columbia that levy separate estate and/or inheritance taxes, there's even more at stake, with death taxes sometimes starting at the first dollar of an estate."

As I don't give tax advice to clients, I always tell the beneficiaries of an inheritance to consult with tax professionals. Often I work directly with these clients and their accountants to make sure that their investments and tax obligations are handled properly.

Resources:

How to Make the Most of an Inheritance and Deal with Estate Tax – If you get an inheritance, one of the first questions you may ask is how to minimize the resulting taxes. In this 8-minute financial podcast, find out what you need to know about maximizing the growth of an inheritance and whether you will face estate tax issues.

What is the Best Way to Invest an Inheritance? If you receive an inheritance, what is the best way to invest it – to pay off debt or put it into savings? On this podcast, follow a six-step plan for updating your portfolio to make the best use of an inheritance.

Go to the free resource page at **www.Profile-Financial.com/inheritancebook** to find the links to these podcasts.

5

The Easy Way to Plan Your Estate

YOU CAN'T TAKE IT WITH YOU

Through the years, you diligently worked to build the assets and save the funds that now represent your net worth. But, when the inevitable occurs, will your money and property be passed on in the manner that you would want? Might the *wrong* person inherit your assets? What will happen to your children? Your spouse? Your business?

WILL YOUR HEIRS HAVE DIFFICULTIES?

When a loved one passes away, many challenges suddenly confront the surviving heirs, no matter the size of the deceased's estate. Who will inherit what? Who will have the authority to continue to run the family business? Is there documentation to prevent an incompetent relative from being put in that position? Who will care for family members with disabilities? How can assets in the deceased's name be made available for the family's immediate use? Who will pay the bills? If young children are suddenly left without parents, who will care for them? Who will handle the money being left for them? Will the funds be immediately turned over to them when they are no longer minors? If your children are already young adults, consider whether they would be ready for this monetary responsibility at their current age. Or would they be better off if you set up a trust for them so that assets would be distributed as needed over a period of time? What if your spouse remarries a person with children and those children wind up becoming your benefactors instead of your own kids? Answers to all these questions have to be carefully considered and legally stated.

Surprisingly, many people don't have up-to-date wills and trusts that spell out their wishes, and this often leads to adverse consequences. If you don't have adequately drawn-up succession documents, a court-appointed attorney may be delegated to process your estate. Will he provide for your heirs as you would have wished? How much will it cost?

Though Israel does not have an estate tax (yet), keep in mind that the United States imposes a graduated "death tax" on its citizens, regardless of whether they live – or die – on American soil or abroad. U.S. estate taxes need to be filed if the estate's combined gross assets and prior taxable gifts exceed $11.2 million in 2018.

UNLIMITED MARITAL INHERITANCE

The American estate tax does not apply to transfers at death from one spouse to another (as long as the recipient is a U.S. citizen). So if an American dies and leaves $50 million to his wife, the money will not be subject to an estate tax. However, when she dies, bequeathing the assets to a non-spouse, the prevailing estate tax will apply. Keep these points in mind. Whether your assets could be subject to a U.S. tax, or to an estate tax Israel might one day enact, you may be able to lessen the blow by establishing proper will and trust documentation now.

BEFORE YOU THINK OF THE HEREAFTER

Lest you get too concerned with asset management after you are gone, remember that it is just as important – if not more so – to address potential problems that may affect your own needs while you are alive. When meeting with your estate planners, discuss the manner in which you would like vital matters to be handled during your lifetime, should you be unable to do so yourself. What would happen if you were unable to adequately function because of mental or physical limitations? Who would make financial decisions for you? Who would make the medical decisions pertaining to your health? A "power of attorney" is the written right that you (the "principal") give to another person to act on your behalf (to be your "attorney-in-fact" or "agent") in specific matters. Various types of clauses and documents may apply under differing circumstances (such as only being applicable if you are alive or only relating to your brokerage accounts). Other instruments, which are broader in scope, may allow discretion in handling all financial matters, including the making of distributions from your trust. Thus, formats can be "limited" (the agent can act only in certain areas) or "general" (the agent can act in all matters). In addition, the power of attorney can be considered "durable" (which means it will remain in effect when/ if the principal becomes incapacitated) or "non-durable" (which limits the scope of the agent's powers and responsibilities).

When sitting down with your lawyer to implement estate-planning documents, it is also imperative to consider health-related proxies. You should select people to make important health-related decisions for you if you should become mentally or physically impaired. In addition to appointing an attorney-in-fact to be responsible for ongoing medical decisions on your behalf, it is also crucial to write a "living will" to address another important related matter: how and whether or not you want medical treatment to be administered or continued if your physical condition is considered terminal with no hope of improvement. If you were to wish to have a "Do not resuscitate" order entered on your medical chart, your agent could present your document to your physician with the request.

WHY DO PEOPLE NEED WILLS AND TRUSTS?

The concept of setting up a trust started in England during the Middle Ages, when knights went off to battle. A departing warrior would entrust his money and property to a friend or to the local church. They agreed to oversee day-to-day affairs, use funds to care for the family, and return the assets to the knight when he came back (or to the knight's children if he didn't return).

Even if you are not about to embark on a crusade, there are nevertheless good reasons for you to write a will and give thought to setting up an appropriate trust. If your assets might be subject to American estate taxes, you might consider initiating a divesting program. In this way, you can give away money during your lifetime as you see fit. This method of disbursement allows you to have full control of where and to whom your money goes and, depending on current tax laws, it might even save on taxes before and after your demise.

BEGIN WITH YOUR WILL

A will is a must-have legally enforceable document that states how you want your assets to be allocated after your death, how you want particular family members cared for, and how other matters relevant to you or to your business should be handled. Your will takes effect when you die. Until then, you can change your will at any time, as you deem appropriate. But upon your demise, the last version, called your "final will and testament," will be legally executed to govern the disposition of your assets and the fulfillment of all your final wishes.

Before you sit down with your lawyer to write your will or to begin thinking about an appropriate trust, make sure you have done some preparation. Organize your paperwork. Review your balance sheets. Look over your assets and liabilities. In addition, consider two points of prime importance: If you have minor children, who should be named guardian? And, who will be the executor of your estate?

WHO WILL CARE FOR YOUR CHILDREN?

If your children are still minors, have a serious discussion with your spouse to consider what would happen to them if either one or both of you were to die or become incapacitated. If you are the main breadwinner and were suddenly no longer around, would your spouse have sufficient funding to carry on? What type of extra help might be needed? Would there be enough assets for tuition, healthcare, weddings, and other important expenses?

While death leaves an emotional void in family life, do what you can to eliminate the risk of a financial void. Then consider the almost unthinkable. What would happen if both you and your spouse were no longer around?

- Who would care for your children?

- Where would they live?

- Who would pay their expenses?

- Are there potential guardians you might consider suitable for the job of raising your kids?

  ○ Are these guardians in sufficiently good health to handle such responsibility?

  ○ Would they bring up your youngsters with the same values you hold dear?

- Should the prospective guardians also have control of the children's assets that you plan to leave for their benefit? Alternatively, should someone else, perhaps a professional trustee, manage the funds?

- What if the logical blood relative choices do not seem genuinely interested in your children's welfare? Or are not fiscally competent? Or do not share your values? Should you look at non–relatives?

- And what if the couple you designate subsequently gets a divorce? What then would happen to the children? It may be wise to give custody to an individual rather than a couple to avoid any confusion.

After finally reaching a decision, your next step would be to discuss the matter with the person or people you wish to name to find out if, in fact, they would agree to the responsibility. Difficult as these judgments are, they are even more complex for parents who are divorced. Legal intervention is often necessary in such cases to determine how the children's needs can best be met.

In Israel, the appointment of guardianship comes from the court. However, generally speaking, your will or letter of intention is taken into consideration. Be sure, therefore, that you have explicitly stated your wishes on this matter and supported your comments with appropriate documentation.

WHO SHOULD BE THE EXECUTOR?

The executor will be responsible for determining and carrying out your wishes after your death, in accordance with the law. When choosing an executor, take into account the person's honesty, decision-making ability, and common sense, as well as his grasp of the world of finance and his willingness to seek out professional help, when and if needed. He should feel comfortable using the services of an attorney, an accountant, a financial advisor, and other experts as he proceeds with the required legal steps. Commonly, spouses, relatives, friends, business associates, bank trustees, personal attorneys, accountants, or financial professionals are chosen to be executors. Alternatively, it can also be an appointee of the court. Whomever you finally settle upon, be sure he is trustworthy and competent enough to carry out a series of duties that must be attended to efficiently and in a timely fashion. Here is a sampling of the many responsibilities that an executor will encounter.

EXECUTORS' TASKS:

1. Locating, assembling, and organizing the assets of the estate.
2. Evaluating the assets (often professional appraisals are required).
3. Identifying which assets will pass through probate and which will pass directly to beneficiaries (e.g., insurance policies and retirement accounts

with listed beneficiaries avoid probate and pass directly).

4. Dealing with probate issues. If your assets are not already in a trust when you die, then your will must be probated in court. Probate enables a judge to ascertain that the will is valid, and allows him to formally appoint the executor. If you have assets in multiple jurisdictions, say a home in Israel, a rental property in New York, and a Florida getaway, your estate may require "ancillary probate," which means that the executor will have to engage in probate proceedings in every state where property is owned. The probate procedure is not confidential (whereas a trust is *not* open to public perusal) and the will itself is available for scrutiny by anyone.

5. Collecting assets owed to the estate and paying off debts, expenses, estate and final personal income taxes, and court and administrative fees for which the estate is responsible. Notifying employers, retirement fund administrators, Social Security, *Bituach Leumi*, and any other issuers of benefit payments. Also, informing issuers of home, car, and other insurance policies to cancel or update policies to reflect new ownership.

6. Temporarily managing the estate's property and liquidating assets when necessary.

7. Keeping a careful accounting of all administrative details.

8. Completing the probate process and then distributing the assets as specified.

If, after considering the above listing, you feel that your executor will need help, or that your estate matters are so complex that it will take more than one person to handle them, consider naming a co-executor – possibly a lawyer or bank trustee – to share the responsibilities. Choosing a professional to be the primary or co-executor of your estate can be advantageous for many reasons. Professionals are knowledgeable in their field and may be able to save money for your estate by doing things right the first time around; they are apt to be impartial when making decisions about your children's welfare; they are up to date with the constantly changing estate laws; and, in the case of bank executors and trustees, they provide your estate with continuity. Professionals will charge a fee that may be based on a percentage of the total estate, on an hourly fee schedule, or on an agreed-upon set amount. Non-professionals may charge a fee, too. It's reasonable to pay someone for the service of being your executor because he will have a great deal of work and responsibility. If payment isn't offered, burdening a family member or friend with the work may be considered unfair. This could lead to a long, drawn-out process as the executor may not make your estate his top priority.

REVIEW AND UPDATE DOCUMENTS REGULARLY

Once you have chosen the guardian for your children and the executor of your estate, and have met with appropriate legal advisors, your work is still not done. You have some very important ongoing obligations: to pay attention to your assets, keep them organized, maintain accurate and current records, and make appropriate document changes when necessary. If you don't, you may inadvertently create nightmares for your heirs. Consider the unfortunate scenario of younger children being left out of receiving the proceeds from an insurance policy taken out before their births (only the older siblings, who had been born already, were listed as beneficiaries). Or, what if a second marriage had occurred and the beneficiary listing wasn't changed from the first spouse to the second? What happens when the chosen executor has become old and frail, and the alternate you so carefully selected has passed away? Periodic review can help avoid situations like these and provide motivation to correct the inequities.

While there are many technicalities involved in preparing estate documents, don't be discouraged from getting started. Remember that careful planning of wills not only eases the emotional angst for the family, but conscientious planning can truly make a long-lasting difference.

WILL OR TRUST?

If you have a will, do you also need a trust? That depends. First of all, to clarify the definitions: A will is a legal document that states a person's final wishes for his assets and dependents. A trust is a relationship that allows one party (the "trustee") to hold property for the benefit of someone else (the "beneficiary"). For some people, especially those who are less affluent, have simple family structures, and don't own a business, a simple will may be quite adequate. For others, a will *and* trust may be the better solution. For these individuals, a "pour-over" will might be worth considering. It allows assets previously not assigned to a trust to be "poured" into the trust upon the estate owner's death. If you have set up a trust and placed most of your assets in it, those assets will avoid probate; however, assets that are dealt with through a "pour-over" will must be probated.

KEEPING YOUR ASSETS IN A TRUST

While trusts are complicated legal documents which should be written by professionals, the vocabulary within them should be understood by everyone involved. In order for a trust to exist, there must be "trust property" (sometimes called the trust "principal" or "corpus"). The creator of the trust (the one who establishes it) is called the "grantor," "settlor," or "trustor." The person who has legal control of the trust's assets is called the "trustee." Anyone who stands to benefit from the trust is called a "beneficiary." Often one person plays more than one role. Thus, a grantor can be a trustee (or co-trustee) and also a beneficiary. Upon creation of the trust, the grantor and the trustee must be legally competent. Trusts are established in different ways, depending on the grantor's goals. When the grantor (settlor) is both the beneficiary and also the trustee, it is important for him to choose a co-trustee or to nominate a subsequent trustee to avoid a court appointment of a trustee upon his death. If the grantor has chosen another person (or institution) as trustee, rather than himself, the trustee will manage the assets and distribute funds in accordance with the trust's regulations. If the trust is a "revocable trust," the settlor retains ultimate control and can replace the trustee if he is dissatisfied. On the other hand, if he establishes an "irrevocable trust," the settlor will have no ongoing say in any matters of the trust, having irrevocably handed over power to someone else.

An example of a common, revocable trust – Since trusts may sound rather complicated for people who haven't considered them before, here's how one could look: Grandpa and Grandma set up a trust naming themselves as trustees and beneficiaries. That means that they control the money in the trust, and they can use the money for themselves. They indicate in the trust document that if they are no longer capable of handling the money, then their son, Sonny, should take over as trustee, but they are still the beneficiaries. That means that if they become incompetent, Sonny will manage the money for the benefit of Grandpa and Grandma. Moreover, they write in the trust document that when they die, Sonny should continue as the trustee and Sonny and his son, Junior, should be beneficiaries. They further dictate that Junior can only use the money from the trust to pay for education and healthcare expense until he is 30 years old.

Once Junior is 30, an age that Grandpa and Grandma consider mature, then he can have access to his share of the funds.

An example of a trust in a divorce situation – Grandpa and Grandma want to leave their money to Sonny, but they don't think that Sonny's marriage will last, and they don't want his wife, Esmerelda, to get any of their money. They write a trust that stipulates that Sonny cannot get any money from the trust while he is married to Esmerelda. In this case, since the money would be the property of the trust, even after Grandpa and Grandma die, Esmerelda could not get her hands on it.

REVOCABLE VS. IRREVOCABLE

For tax purposes, one of the most important characteristics of a trust is whether it is revocable (which means the settlor can take back all the assets into his own name) or irrevocable (which means the settlor permanently and completely gives his assets to the trust). Generally, if a trust is revocable, the government will view it as just another account belonging to the settlor. That's fine if you, as the settlor, are trying to avoid having your assets go through probate. However, if you are attempting to lower your tax obligations by placing your assets in a revocable trust, you will not accomplish this goal. The government takes the position that since you have easy access to the funds, you should pay any applicable taxes on them.

On the opposite side of the spectrum is the person who irrevocably gives money to a trust with no strings attached. It's as if he gave a gift to someone else. Should the government be able to claim that the donor has to pay tax on money that he no longer has, nor controls, nor benefits from? Determining the exact tax status of an irrevocable trust is a complicated question. Many people believe that they've established irrevocable trusts and think the money therein has escaped the reach of the taxman; but sometimes they are wrong. Beware – if you have any incidence of ownership; if you have any decision-making power over the money; if you stand to benefit from the assets; if you can write a check or use a debit card from the trust's bank account; or even if you can exert influence over someone else who controls the trust – the irrevocable status of your trust might be disqualified by the tax authority of Israel, the United States, or both. Then, all the assets would be considered yours for tax purposes. This is especially detrimental when a U.S. citizen is trying to get assets out of his own name before he dies to avoid having them become subject to the estate tax. Due to the complexities involved in estate planning, when creating a trust, make sure you get experienced, qualified tax and legal advice. Your trust has to work right the first time around. You don't get a second chance.

SHOULD YOU SET UP A TRUST?

Trusts vary in focus and intent. Couples with children often set up revocable living trusts (also known as "*inter vivos*" trusts) to protect and benefit their families in the future. They retain control of the trust property by being both the grantors and the trustees, and can therefore withdraw assets to use for current needs and wants. While they're alive, the trust's earnings are taxed as if they were the earnings of the grantors. In effect, the tax code makes no differentiation between the grantors' individual assets and those of the trust. When the grantors die, the assets in the trust will normally avoid probate (many people find probate a hassle) and will move smoothly along as per the document's instructions.

To determine if a trust might benefit you and your family, consider a few of the compelling reasons why people choose to create them:

- An income stream can be established for minor children and/or other heirs.

- Adult children who are unprepared to manage a large sum of money can receive funds at specified intervals or when certain milestones are achieved, like graduating college or reaching a specified age.

- Assets can be protected from creditors. For example, instead of bequeathing money to children who are in professions where they might get sued (i.e., the medical profession) the money could remain in a trust, out of reach of potential creditors. (Since this is a tricky issue, make sure a qualified lawyer designs your trust.)

- Probate can be avoided.

- Family finances can be kept confidential.

- Certain tax benefits can be achieved.

COMMON TRUST CONCEPTS

Trusts should be personalized to meet specific needs. There are many options available. The specific format of a trust can be designed to protect the grantor, beneficiary, or both. Below are some varieties of trusts and provisions commonly used in the U.S. If you are unsure of your category or what your needs really are, speak with a professional. Also, note that Israeli trust concepts differ from the American legal viewpoint. After you have developed a plan to achieve your goals with a U.S. trust, go over it with an Israeli trust expert to make sure that you have not inadvertently created more problems than you're solving.

Discretionary provisions in a trust allow the trustees, as they see fit, to distribute interest and/or principal to the beneficiaries. Sometimes a trust includes a term called a "sprinkling" or "spray" provision, which narrows the discretionary powers of the trustees so that they can only distribute income from dividends and interest (not principal) as they deem reasonable.

Special needs trusts deal with people whose situation is beyond the norm, especially in the case of a handicapped family member. For example, some disabled people receive government aid. However, their public assistance could be cut if they were to receive an inheritance, even a small one. To provide help for disabled children and other dependent beneficiaries, while not limiting the other income streams available to them, special needs trusts may be used.

A *Generation Skipping Trust* (GST) is ideal for people who believe in thinking far ahead. Also known as a "dynasty trust," this vehicle allows wealthy individuals to pass their assets to their grandchildren in a tax-saving manner. Ordinarily, if the money is passed to the children of the deceased, it would be subject to estate taxes. Then, when these individuals died, the money would be passed on to their children (the original donor's grandchildren) and the funds could be taxed again. The GST allows a specified amount of money to be set aside in order to avoid double taxation.

Spendthrift provisions in a trust prohibit the transfer of the beneficiary's rights in the trust to anyone else. In principle, a beneficiary who is entitled to income from a trust could transfer his rights to the income stream from the trust to a third party. This means that a trust beneficiary who racks up excessive gambling debts, for example, might be able to sign over his future income from the trust to the loan shark to whom he owes money. If the trust has a spendthrift clause, however, the trustees could refuse to disseminate any funds that would go to settle that debt. Similarly, if an unfortunate trust beneficiary drives himself out of business and is stuck with a lot of debts, the trustees can refuse to pay off the creditors.

An *incentive trust* can help to compel the beneficiaries to achieve certain goals before they can receive funds.

Distributions may be tied to the beneficiary taking certain actions, such as finishing university, entering a profession, starting a business, or getting married. Incentives must be legal in order to eliminate a court overturning them one day. They are usually used to make sure that trust beneficiaries don't become "trust brats." Billionaire Sam Walton (founder of Wal-Mart) spelled out the philosophy that many trust makers follow when he said that he would leave his children enough money so that they could do anything, but not so much that they could do nothing.

Charitable Remainder Trusts (**CRTs**) provide assistance to qualified charities and simultaneously benefit the donors. A highly appreciated asset (i.e., one that if sold now would be subject to a lot of capital gains tax) can be placed into this type of irrevocable trust. By doing so, you would not have to pay capital gains tax on the amount that this asset (stock, home, art collection, etc.) appreciated since you originally acquired it. And, you would receive an immediate income-tax deduction for the contribution (the amount of which depends on various factors that you should review with your accountant). In addition to these tax savings, the donation would no longer be considered as your asset and thus would not be included in your estate (and not subject to any applicable inheritance tax). It is possible to design the trust so that even though the assets do not belong to you, you could receive a certain lifetime income from the trust. When you die, the charity would get to keep the asset.

A *Qualified Terminable Interest Property Trust* (**QTIP**) allows assets to eventually be distributed in accordance with the written wishes of the spouse who set it up. It stipulates that should this spouse die first, the surviving spouse will receive the ongoing income and a percent of the principal, but upon his or her death, the *corpus* (i.e., principal) will pass on to the heirs chosen by the first spouse. Under the guidelines of the QTIP trust, taxes are deferred until the death of the surviving spouse. QTIP trusts are most often used when there are children from a previous marriage. Even if there are not, some people use this trust to prevent a future spouse of the survivor from having access to, or wasting the estate funds.

A *Qualified Domestic Trust* (**QDOT**) addresses the problem of transferring assets to a non-citizen spouse who may not qualify for a marital deduction. For example, a U.S. citizen with a $40 million estate could marry another U.S. citizen and bequeath the whole sum to her upon his death with no estate (death) taxes.

If he married an Israeli, though, there would be estate tax issues as the money passes to his non-U.S. wife. The rules require a U.S. trustee to ensure collection of the death tax upon the demise of the surviving spouse. Speak to a qualified estate attorney if this is applicable to your situation.

NOT ALL TRUSTS ARE SUITABLE

A common misconception is that one can avoid taxes by putting assets in a trust. In some ways this may be true, but be aware that trusts themselves are subject to taxes, and sometimes at higher tax rates than are individuals. While trusts can provide some tax savings and cut probate-related expenses, they do not necessarily offer savings when it comes to estate or income taxes. Various financial "experts" sometimes suggest certain new or impressive trust strategies that provide tax savings. Use caution when listening to their advice since there are no magic trust solutions. For example, offshore schemes aimed at hiding money may well lead to misery. (*Hiding* money is not a tax-planning technique. It is tax evasion and, needless to say, illegal.)

DO YOU NEED EXPERT ADVICE?

Although you may be a jack-of-all-trades, it is generally not a good idea to handle your will and trust-making activities by yourself. No matter the size of your estate, it's in your own interest to have highly competent advisors on your side, helping you to manage your assets appropriately. Choose professionals who are experts in their fields, keep up to date with the latest rules and information, are willing to take time to let you express your concerns and hopes, and are available to you when you need them. Ideally, your professional advisors will not only work with you on a one-to-one basis but also will consult and work with each other on your behalf.

WHO WILL BE ON YOUR ADVISORY TEAM?

Your goal is to find highly qualified people who are knowledgeable in their field, intelligent, diligent, honest, and truly interested in helping you to accomplish your objectives. Ask acquaintances whose judgment you respect for references. Arrange meetings with the candidates you are considering and see how the interaction goes. Do you clearly understand what they are talking about? Do they listen carefully to your responses and opinions? Do you have confidence in their knowledge? Ask about their credentials and experience. When you feel comfortable with the answers, continue by asking about fees. Be wary of advisors who try to rush you into making a decision, who make you a now-or-never offer, who are more interested in bragging about themselves than in learning about you, and who forget – or are too busy to return your calls.

Financial advisor. Professional financial planners are skilled in helping people analyze their needs and aspirations. They can show clients how to coordinate their goals with the reality of their finances. Often financial planners work with multiple generations in the same family and help heirs understand their new economic situation. If assets must be liquidated to pay estate-related taxes and debts, they can offer counsel on which holdings would be suitable choices for selling. Frequently, a financial planner is also a fully licensed stockbroker and can provide in-depth advice on various investments as well as help in expediting transference of holdings in the account to beneficiaries upon receipt of the required documentation. (If there are still stock certificates in someone's name when he passes on, the executor will have to deal with the various corporate transfer agents and send each of them the required forms and a copy of the death certificate in order to have the shares reassigned to the beneficiaries.)

When checking out planners, ask some of these questions: Are they licensed in the countries where they do business? Are they Certified Financial Planner™ practitioners (accredited by the CFP board, which affirms their high level of achievement in financial education, experience, and ethics)? Are they Registered Investment Advisors (who have passed the required testing and are registered with the U.S. Securities and Exchange Commission [SEC] as investment advisors)? Are they certified TEPs (members of the Society of Trust and Estate Practitioners [STEP], an organization of highly experienced experts in the field of taxes, trusts, and estates)?

Financial advisors can help families before, during, and after the estate-settling process. Because they are familiar with the overall financial picture, financial advisors are often the central hub of an advisory team – the coordinators of the group of professionals.

Accountant. These professionals contribute to the advisory team by recommending tax-efficient ways to help the client set up his estate-planning documents and process tax-related forms. When there are choices to make, they explain the consequences and potential ramifications of the various alternatives to the heirs. An accountant can answer questions pertaining to filing the current year's taxes on behalf of the deceased. Perhaps a comprehensive review might be required in preparing final documentation. Tax issues might also arise regarding assets and tax rules in different countries. What are the implications for Americans living in Israel? What happens with regard to taxes when *olim* inherit money from abroad?

Estate-planning attorney. This specially trained lawyer uses proper legal forms and tax-efficient methods to help clients draw up their wills and trust documents to arrange for the transfer of assets from one generation to the next. When the time comes, if the executor requires ongoing help, the attorney can continue to assist and provide guidance in settling the estate. In America, families frequently turn to lawyers for this kind of help in handling their estates. However, in Israel, where probate usually entails only minimal costs, and where there is currently no inheritance tax to contend with, it is less common.

Trust officer. If the deceased chose a bank or trust company to be the fiduciary/executor of his will and/or trust, the officer of the chosen institution would meet with the heirs and handle the estate settlement procedure for them in a manner that complies with the wishes of the grantor. And, if it was stated in the trust documents, the trust officer (and the institution) would continue the relationship with the heirs by serving as a trustee (or co-trustee).

Development officer. Many people feel that in addition to providing for their heirs, they also wish to pass on assets to a favorite charitable institution. Others want to contribute even before they are gone so that their assets can help even sooner. And still others, knowing of the potential tax and income benefits that can accrue from a major donation in the form of a charitable remainder trust, decide to follow the path of philanthropy. When a contributor is considering a major gift, he should speak with the charity's development officer who can provide appropriate information and help arrange the paperwork.

Insurance agent. Experienced agents or planners can help people decide which types of coverage they should carry to supplement their work-related policies. Insurance agents can help clients determine how much insurance they should have in case they become ill, sustain a disability, or die. How much business insurance should a person carry? How about malpractice insurance? Homeowners insurance? Liability insurance? Life insurance? In whose names should the various policies be? Who should be the beneficiaries? Can the way in which individuals establish their policies affect their taxes? Which companies offer the best coverage at the best prices? These are questions that an insurance agent can help answer.

Guest articles by
Russell D. Mayer, Adv.

Russell Mayer is one of the senior partners of the law firm Livnat Mayer & Co., which he founded in 1998. Originally from New York, but now living in Israel, Mr. Mayer received his J.D. degree from the Benjamin N. Cardozo School of Law at Yeshiva University and is a member of both the Israel Bar and New York State Bar Associations. He deals with corporate and commercial law, elder care, wills and estates, real estate, finance and trade law, labor law, intellectual property law, and more. He has contributed to various publications, including legal articles and columns to the *Times of Israel* newspaper, YNET online newspaper, and *Connections Magazine*.

Mr. Mayer can be reached at www.LMF.co.il or by phone, from Israel: 02-679-9533 or from the U.S.: 1-202-470-4007.

6

Israeli Ongoing Power of Attorney and Other Documents

By Russell D. Mayer, Adv. (Updated information as of January, 2018. Reprinted with permission.)

In 2017, Israel took an evolutionary leap forward in anticipating and addressing the needs of the elderly and others who may become incapacitated, by adopting Amendment 18 of the Legal Capacity and Guardianship Law, 5722-1962 (the "Law"). The revisions to the law are intended to empower individuals, not only the elderly, by giving them the ability to determine their own destiny with respect to their care and the management of their affairs. The Law fills a dual gap in Israeli practice to date: (a) the lack of an Israeli equivalent to a Durable Power of Attorney (which continues to be effective once the grantor is no longer mentally capable) and (b) preserving the independence and self-respect of those who suffer from diminished capacity.

Until the Amendment came into effect this year, an Israeli Power of Attorney would generally lapse once a person would become mentally incompetent, at which point a guardian would need to be appointed by the Court to care for the person's finances. Furthermore, there was no mechanism in place to allow individuals to choose the person who would become their guardian so that the decision was left solely to the discretion of the Court. The new documents complete a comprehensive set of procedures which will allow those who choose to adopt at least some of these choices to determine their own care. In addition to a properly executed Last Will and Testament, the documents which one should consider executing while one has the mental capacity to do so, are as follows:

1. "Regular" Power of Attorney. Powers of Attorney done outside of Israel will generally NOT be recognized in Israel. An Israeli regular Power of Attorney, which must be signed in the pres-

ence of an Israeli Notary, gives the authority to another person to act on your behalf in most cases only as long as you are mentally competent. It is useful in the event that you become physically incapacitated, unable to go to the bank or post office, or otherwise manage your affairs at a time when you are immobile. Unlike a Durable Power of Attorney, a regular Power of Attorney ceases to be effective once a person is no longer mentally competent. Again, a Durable Power of Attorney done outside of Israel will generally not be recognized for use in Israel.

2. Ongoing Power of Attorney. This document supplements a regular power of attorney as it provides a legal mechanism which fills the gap between not having a regular power of attorney in place and the ultimate appointment of a guardian by the court. It is designed to come into effect specifically once a person is no longer competent whether due to age, Alzheimer's, an accident or otherwise. The Ongoing Power of Attorney allows individuals to determine their own future course of care – whether regarding their possessions, person, living arrangements or otherwise. It further empowers the grantor to cancel authority previously given. The intention

behind the change is to grant people more autonomy in crafting their futures, to preserve their dignity and express their preferences – while they are still in a position to do so. An individual may, while still competent, execute an Ongoing Power of Attorney allowing him or herself to decide in advance:

- under what conditions the authority will become effective (e.g., as determined by an expert, upon a certain event, or at a particular date).

- who will be authorized to act at that time on behalf of the individual.

- whether the authority will apply to managing possessions, the person, medical decisions, or even business.

- whether the individual can exclude or limit the various authorities granted.

- whether the individual would be allowed to rescind the authority in the future or whether it would lapse should certain conditions apply.

- who would be appointed guardian if or when it becomes necessary.

- whether the "proxy holder" (the person who is given power of attorney) would be able to have the individual committed to an institution or require him to undergo a psychiatric evaluation, or arrange for release from commitment.

- who is to be notified at the time that the authority is being triggered.

- who is authorized to see the details of the Ongoing Power of Attorney.

- appointment of a replacement guardian for guardianship – if the primary guardian is not willing or able to serve (for instance, if Chaim is a guardian for Shmuel, to appoint Reuven to replace Chaim if Chaim is not willing or able to serve).

- appointment of a healthcare proxy which is a separate document referenced below and is NOT covered by the Ongoing Power of Attorney (although it is referenced in the document if it has been issued previously).

The Ongoing Power of Attorney may only be prepared and executed under the supervision of an Israeli lawyer who has been specially trained for this purpose by the Administrator General ("Specially Trained and Authorized Israeli Lawyer"). There are only a limited number of Israeli lawyers who have received the certification. (The author of this article, Russell D. Mayer, is a Specially Trained and Authorized Israeli Lawyer at Livnat Mayer & Co.)

3. Choosing a Guardian. Yet another new provision in the Law allows an individual to designate in advance who would ultimately be appointed as Guardian if or when it becomes necessary. This document must also be prepared and executed under the supervision of one of the Specially Trained and Authorized Israeli Lawyers.

4. Healthcare Proxy. The revisions to the Law adopted a new form of Healthcare Proxy together with the new obligation to file the Healthcare Proxy with the office of the Administrator General. The Healthcare Proxy allows people to choose who will be authorized to make medical decisions on their behalf if they are unable to make their own decisions at that time (due to temporary or other incapacity, unconsciousness, while undergoing an operation or otherwise). The document must be witnessed by one of five professionals (doctor, lawyer, nurse,

social worker, or psychologist) who certifies on the document that the person giving, as well as the person accepting, the authority are mentally competent at the time of signing and understood the ramifications of the document. The Healthcare Proxy does NOT address end-of-life decisions.

5. Living Will. The Living Will, or as technically referred to the "Advanced Directive for a Dying Patient" is the document in which an individual can, in advance, make end-of-life care decisions. It is a detailed document which has numerous choices for individuals to determine what types of treatments they want or don't want to receive at a time when they have been certified as "dying" (akin to "under hospice care"). The document must include the certification of the patient's regular doctor as to the medical condition of the patient at the time of signing and the doctor is to explain to the patient the ramifications of the numerous choices available. Signature on the document must be witnessed by two witnesses.

6. The Law also provides for the selection of a "supporter" who would assist the individual in making decisions during the difficult transition time

between being fully competent and once the individual becomes incompetent.

———

This memorandum is not to be considered as a legal opinion. For legal advice, contact legal counsel directly.

7

What You Need to Know About Writing a Will

By Russell D. Mayer, Adv. (Reprinted with permission.)

───────

As it says in *Kohelet* (*Ecclesiastes*), there is a time for everything. Planning for the inevitable, therefore, makes good sense.

What arrangements can be made in a will? Does it matter if you already have a will that you executed abroad? What happens if you don't have a will? Who takes care of your children when you die? Who gets your prized possessions when you die? Is it really necessary to engage an attorney to draft your will?

GENERAL RULES

INHERITANCE

Israeli inheritance laws govern the distribution of a deceased's property located in Israel. The law pertains to distribution of assets in the absence of a legally valid will ("intestate") as well as the rules applicable to preparing and executing a will.

In the absence of a legally binding will, a deceased's spouse would receive all movable property (including a car) owned by the deceased at the time of his or her death. With respect to the remaining assets: (a) if the deceased had children, then the spouse would receive half of the remainder and the children or their descendants would receive the balance (equal shares to each of the children or their descendants) or (b) if the deceased had no children but left a surviving spouse and siblings, then the spouse would receive two-thirds of the remainder with the balance divided among the siblings.

Outside of Israel, certain types of joint ownership will automatically convey the deceased's share to the surviving joint owner regardless of intestate succession or provisions of a will. In such cases, regardless of what it says in the will, the property of the deceased will pass automatically to the survivor. In Israel, the presumption is that each joint owner of an asset, such as a bank account or an apartment, is owned proportionately by the owners and does NOT pass to the other joint owner(s) upon the demise of one of them. It is necessary to get a Court order to transfer the interests of the deceased either according to the deceased's will, or if there is no will, according to the rules of intestacy as explained above. It is therefore important, in the course of planning one's estate, to share with your lawyer a thorough description of all assets held by the parties as well as the technical title so that the lawyer can advise how to structure the estate passing under the will while taking into consideration assets that may pass outside of it.

Section 17(a) of the Inheritance Law, 5725-1965 (the "Law") provides that where an heir cannot otherwise be identified pursuant to the Law, the State of Israel shall inherit the estate.

GUARDIANSHIP

Israel's guardianship law, the Legal Capacity and Guardianship Law, 5722-1962, determines who will be appointed as guardian of minor children or incapacitated individuals. The State's Administrator General (*"apotropos haklali"*) will often take the totality of circumstances into consideration in determining who is best suited to be appointed guardian. In the absence of a surviving parent, the State guardian will give preference to immediate relatives (e.g., parents' siblings, parents, aunts and uncles). If a parent stipulates the appointment of a specific guardian in a will, the Administrator General and the courts will generally respect that provision. It is, therefore, highly recommended that one provide for the appointment of guardianship of minors in a will and that the appointment be made within the parameters of the law.

ISRAELI INHERITANCE TAX

Israel had an inheritance tax until several years ago. From time to time the tax authorities suggest that they are considering reintroducing the tax. Until such time as the tax is re-implemented, tax considerations which may have been considered in developing a will abroad, may not be applicable regarding Israeli assets (although they may still be subject to foreign inheritance taxes). Therefore, inheritance plans in Israel may have more flexibility than those done in other countries. It is, however, important to take into consideration the tax regimes to which the individual may be subject (e.g., U.S. inheritance tax for U.S. cit-

izens even if they live outside of the United States –
the Federal exemption for U.S. citizens' inheritance
tax as of January 1, 2018 is $11.2 million per person).

PROBATE

A will generally needs to be processed (e.g., probated)
in every jurisdiction in which assets are located (e.g.,
if there is one will and assets in both Israel and the
U.S., probate will need to be done in both countries).

TRUSTS

Particularly if minors are involved, immediately or
potentially, a properly executed will, which should be
drafted by an experienced attorney, may very well
include the establishment of trusts that will control
the use of assets which would otherwise be directly
bequeathed to minors. In other words, for example, a
will might state that rather than giving assets directly
to a child, the money will instead be held in a trust
to be handled for the benefit of the child until a certain age. That trust, which is specified by the will, is
known as a "testamentary trust."

WILLS GENERALLY

A Last Will and Testament (i.e., "will") is an instru-
ment through which testators seek to determine the

method and arrangements for handling their interests upon their demise. A will seeks to supersede the default provisions of intestate succession with the "will" of the testator. There are significant rules and regulations regarding the extent to which intestate succession (default statutory provisions) can be substituted in a will as well as intricate rules involving its proper execution. Mistakes in either of these crucial components can frustrate the intentions of the testator making the will either worthless or harmful to the testator's actual intent. Designing a will (e.g., estate planning) as well as writing and executing a will should only be undertaken by a qualified, knowledgeable lawyer who is experienced in these matters.

Like all written agreements, the clearer the terms and conditions in the will, the less is the likelihood that there will be misunderstanding or that someone will successfully contest its legality. Specificity in the will can communicate the testator's intentions and avoid disputes among the heirs. Actual and emotional value, tax ramifications, and legal constraints should be considered in designing a personal will appropriate for the circumstances.

SOUND MIND AND BODY

In order for a will to be binding, it must be executed at a time that its maker was of sound mind and body. The law determines that a will made by (a) a minor; or (b) a person who has been declared incapacitated/incompetent; or (c) where the will was made at a time when the testator did not distinguish or comprehend the nature of the will, is invalid.

JURISDICTION

Israeli courts have jurisdiction to adjudicate cases (whether for probating a will or under circumstances of intestate succession) if, at the time of his death, the deceased had been domiciled in Israel or left assets in Israel. Domicile will be determined based on the "center of life" of the individual. Citizenship is not necessarily relevant. It will be necessary to apply to the Israeli court in the event that the deceased left assets in Israel even if a will is probated in a court abroad.

TYPES OF WILLS

The most common form of will is the "Printed Will Executed in the Presence of Witnesses." Other types of wills which may be valid under specific, limited circumstances include: (a) handwritten wills, (b) wills executed in the presence of certain officials, and (c) oral wills. It is critical to understand that the requirements for all of these wills are quite intricate and it is easy to inadvertently err in their execution causing the entire will to be considered invalid and unenforceable. Make sure to prepare a will with a lawyer who is competent in this area of the law.

With regard to the U.S. and Israel, a will properly prepared and executed in one county will likely be effective in the other and may be written in English or Hebrew. After the maker passes away, it will likely be necessary to translate the will with notarial certification into the language of the country for which it is not in the native language. For that reason, it may be advantageous to have a separate will for assets in Israel (even though a U.S. will would be recognized in Israel) as U.S. wills tend to be more lengthy and, therefore, more expensive to translate and certify, not to mention that they tend not to have the specificity of identifying heirs as currently required by Israeli law and procedure.

———

This memorandum is not to be considered as a legal opinion. For legal advice, contact legal counsel directly.

Appendix A

Checklists

Throughout the book, the checklists include explanations to make them more understandable. If you want to use the checklists in dealing with your own situation, here they are in abbreviated form. You can also download and print copies at:

www.Profile-Financial.com/inheritancebook.

* * *

CHECKLIST A – PAPERWORK YOU NEED TO CLAIM YOUR INHERITANCE

- Apply to the Israeli Inheritance Registrar for a probate order, even if you live abroad, as Israel doesn't recognize foreign court orders. When applying for a probate order at the Inheritance Registrar in Israel, the following documents need to be presented:

  - An official application for a probate order, if signed in Israel, in the presence of an Israeli lawyer and if signed abroad, then with the certification of the consulate or a notary with Apostille certification.

  - Power of Attorney if your lawyer is making the application on your behalf (same means of witnessing the signing as above).

  - Death certificate.

  - Original will – if signed abroad, often together with an Israeli notarial translation.

  - Signed authorization from your fellow heirs (if there are any) that you are making this application, or an official notice to them that the proceeding is being commenced. The official notification needs to include a copy of the will, with a copy of the dispatch of the documents by registered mail.

- ◦ If the deceased lived outside Israel, the legal opinion of an Israeli lawyer with respect to the applicable foreign law regarding the inheritance.

- If any of the assets are located in the United States, file for a probate order in America.

- If you hire a lawyer to do probate for an Israeli will, but you are not located in Israel, you will need to sign a power of attorney either in the Israeli consulate or in the presence of a notary who must put Apostille certification on the document.

- If the deceased had brokerage or bank accounts in the United States, you will need to obtain:

  - ◦ Original Affidavit of Domicile.

  - ◦ Consular Report of Death of a U.S. Citizen Abroad. To obtain an official copy of the Report of Death, the deceased's legal representative must provide to the U.S. Consulate:

    - ▪ DS 2060 form,

- Original local death certificate,

- The deceased's American passport,

- The deceased's Social Security Number,

- A copy of your passport (if you are the next of kin),

- A notice of death by the hospital or a physician, mentioning the cause of death.

○ Transfer Certificate. Documents you will need to file a request for a transfer certificate include:

- Either (a) State Department Form DS-2060, Report of the Death of an American Citizen, or (b) death certificate and a copy of the photo page of the decedent's current U.S. passport or other proof of U.S. citizenship.

- An affidavit, which is a written declaration made under oath before a notary public or other comparable local official. The affidavit may be in the form of a letter. It must be signed by the executor, administrator or other personal representative of the estate and include (a) a listing of all assets worldwide in which the decedent had any interest at the date of death together with their values on that date, and (b) all taxable gifts made by the decedent after 1976.

- One copy of each inventory filed with domestic or foreign probate authorities, with English translations if in another language.

- One copy of each death tax or inheritance tax return and any corrective statements filed with taxing authorities other than the United States, with English translations if in another language. If the decedent's country of residence does not have a death tax or inheritance tax (as in Israel), provide a copy of the decedent's last income tax return, and a copy of any wealth tax return filed.

- Copies of the decedent's last will and testament along with any codicils, with English translations if in another language.

In order to help you comply with the IRS requirements, prepare the following:

- List of worldwide assets and their value at the date of death,

- Bank statements as of the date of death and as of current date,

- Brokerage statements as of the date of death and as of current date,

- Value of all real estate as of the date of death,

- Value of all other assets as of the date of death, including pensions, *Keren Hishtalmut, Kupot Gemel*, property, etc.,

- Copies of any U.S. gift tax returns from after 1976, if applicable.

If the deceased's estate is worth over $11.2 million (as of 2018), the IRS requires you to also file:

- Form 706, United States Estate Tax Return, together with the supporting documents specified in the Form 706 Instructions.

- Either (a) State Department Form DS-2060, which is the Report of the Death of an American Citizen, or (b) death certificate and a copy of the photo page of the decedent's current U.S. passport or other proof of U.S. citizenship.

———

APPENDIX A

Neither Profile Investment Services, Ltd. nor Portfolio Resources Group, Inc. provide legal advice. This document is intended as general information only about the many steps and documents that may be required to claim an inheritance. You should not depend on this information alone since rules and requirements may change. You should consult an attorney for help with the legal requirements involved in claiming an inheritance.

CHECKLIST B – EXECUTOR'S TASKS

Anyone who is – or may be one day – an executor should know the duties of the job. This is an abbreviated version of the list that appears in Chapter 5 of *The Inheritance Book*. An executor's responsibilities include:

- Locating, assembling, and organizing the assets of the estate,

- Evaluating the assets (or hiring a professional to do the evaluation),

- Identifying which assets will pass through probate and which will pass directly to beneficiaries,

- Dealing with probate issues,

- Collecting assets owed to the estate and paying off debts, expenses, estate and final personal income taxes, and court and administrative fees for which the estate is responsible,

- Notifying employers, retirement fund administrators, Social Security, *Bituach Leumi*, and any other issuers of benefit payments,

- Informing issuers of home, car, and other insurance policies to cancel or update policies to reflect new ownership,

- Temporarily managing the estate's property,

- Liquidating assets when necessary,

- Keeping a careful accounting of all administrative details, and

- Completing the probate process and then distributing the assets as specified.

CHECKLIST C – REASONS TO SET UP A TRUST

This is an abbreviated version of the list that appears in Chapter 5 of *The Inheritance Book*.

- An income stream can be established for minor children and/or other heirs.

- Adult children who are unprepared to manage a large sum of money can receive funds at specified intervals.

- Assets can be protected from creditors.

- Probate can be avoided.

- Family finances can be kept confidential.

- Certain tax benefits can be achieved.

CHECKLIST D – 5 IMPORTANT POINTS FOR WRITING A WILL

- Work with a lawyer who understands the law wherever you have assets and wherever you have citizenship. If you try to save money by doing it all yourself, you may be setting your heirs up for trouble – and for huge legal expenses.

- Name an executor. No law requires you to name an executor in your will, and some lawyers discourage it. An executor is the person who's in charge of making sure the terms of the will are carried out in accordance with the wishes of the deceased. When a will has a named executor, the process goes more smoothly for the heirs.

- *Don't* include account numbers. Some people include specific account numbers in their will thinking that after they die, it will help the executor to find the money. They forget to realize that banks and brokerage firms sometimes change their numbering systems, and that they themselves may also move their money from one firm to another. If you want to be helpful, keep an updated list of all of your accounts, their numbers, and a contact person at the firm, *next* to your will, but not as *part* of your will.

- Ask yourself if you are being fair. Unless there is some very compelling reason, try to distribute your assets equally among your children. People who don't do this often cause animosity among the heirs, which is not a legacy anyone wants to leave.

- Write a will. This checklist presumes that you're writing a will, but unfortunately a lot of people don't. They imagine that it will all work out, but that's not always the case. Lack of a will can cause inconvenience, unnecessary legal expense, and hard feelings. And even worse, if you don't specify in a will what you would like to have happen with your assets, it's possible that your personal goals will not be remembered, understood, or followed. Writing a will does not require a lot of effort, and everyone should do it.

Don't assume that what you are reading here is legal advice. This information is based on the experience of dealing with inheritances from the point of view of an investment advisor, and should not to be taken as legal advice. For that, speak with a competent, licensed professional.

CHECKLIST E – THE DIFFICULT FIRST STEPS OF WIDOWHOOD

- Understand the emotional stages through which people go when dealing with loss.

  - Shock

  - Uncertainty

  - Anger

  - Guilt

  - Loneliness

  - Acceptance

- Focus on immediate practical needs, and ask for help if necessary. Now is the time to call upon friends and family for assistance.

  - Get a notebook to keep track of everything going on.

  - Make funeral/*shiva.*

  - Confirm you have sufficient cash flow.

  - Check that you have access to cash in the bank.

- ○ Review investment statements and records (call a professional if necessary) to see if anything needs immediate attention.

- ○ Find a lawyer to help settle the estate.

- ○ Apply for benefits like pensions, veteran's benefits, Social Security, *Bituach Leumi*.

- ○ Check on your healthcare coverage.

- Put assets in your own name (or in a trust if your lawyer advises) so you have control. In order to file insurance claims, change account names, and apply for benefits, you will need some or all of these documents:

- ○ Original death certificates (order more than you think you'll need)

- ○ Letter of Testamentary – sometimes called a "Letter of Administration" or "Letter of Representation"(document from a local court stating that you are the legal executor for a particular estate)

- ○ Deceased's will

- ○ Deceased's birth certificate

- ○ Marriage certificate

- Social Security number of the deceased

- Joint tax returns for the previous five years

- Records of employee benefits, including retirement plans and stock option plans

- Insurance policies

- Proof of ownership of property (deeds, mortgage statements, titles)

- Car titles, registrations, and related paperwork

- Financial statements (banks, brokerage firms, mutual funds, IRAs, 401(k), retirement accounts, credit card statements)

• Financial plans and portfolios should be handled soon, but in most cases there is no hurry, so take time to deal with them thoughtfully.

- Review your budget.

- Determine all of your sources of income.

- Decide on your most important financial goals.

- Update your financial plan.

- Revise your investment portfolio to reflect your new situation.

Appendix B

How to Open a U.S. Brokerage Account from Overseas

WHO NEEDS A U.S. BROKERAGE ACCOUNT?

From all of the calls and emails I get from around the world, it seems to me that a lot of people want to have a U.S. brokerage account. If you're not sure of the benefits of having a U.S. brokerage account when you live abroad, read, "6 Reasons You Should Have a U.S. Brokerage Account," which you can download for free at: **www.Profile-Financial.com/inheritancebook**. However, the article below is a "how to," and it's meant to help you open a U.S. brokerage account quickly and easily.

THIS ARTICLE WILL HELP YOU IF...

- If you are a U.S. citizen living outside the United States, you may have found that your U.S. bank or brokerage firm has asked you to leave. One of the most common sources of new business for me is when someone walks into my office with a note from a major U.S. firm and he says something like, "Doug, I've had my account with them for over 20 years, and now they sent me this letter saying that I have to close it within 30 days!"

- If you are a non-U.S. citizen who wants to benefit from having a U.S. brokerage account, I'll show you some important facts you should know.

- If you want to own U.S. securities like stocks or bonds but your non-U.S. bank/brokerage firm refuses to assist you. Thousands of banks and investment companies around the world have stopped doing business with Americans because they are afraid of the new FATCA regulations which, according to the IRS, stipulate that "[foreign financial institutions] that do not both register and agree to report [to the IRS] face a 30% withholding tax on certain U.S.-source payments made to them." A bank in England or Germany, for example, with no ties to the United States, now has to send reports about their American clients to the United States Government! Many of these banks feel that the IRS has overstepped its boundaries and are refusing to work with American citizens.

DON'T READ THIS ARTICLE IF...

If you're a money launderer, terrorist, or another sort of bad guy looking to clean up your funds through a U.S. brokerage account, forget it! The compliance officers are well trained to spot miscreants and stop them, so don't bother reading any further. This article is meant for normal folks who want to build up savings for retirement and perhaps create a legacy for future generations, and who intend to follow all applicable laws.

10 STEPS TO OPENING A U.S. BROKERAGE ACCOUNT FOR NON-U.S. RESIDENTS

1. Contact a U.S. brokerage firm that specifically focuses on people residing outside the United States. Though many investment companies won't work with U.S. expats or NRA's (non-resident aliens), many will. If a company seems unfriendly toward you because you have a non-U.S. address, keep looking until you find a firm

that will be happy to open a U.S. brokerage account for you, even though your address is not within the borders of the fifty States. (Our company is one that welcomes such accounts. If you'd like to see what services we can provide for you, go to **www.Profile-Financial.com**).

2. Be prepared to clearly identify yourself. One of the things that brokerage firms must check about their clients is their identity. The best way for you to help confirm your identity is to provide a copy of your passport or any other government-issued identification. The firm will often ask for a copy of a utility bill sent to you at your home address. This will prove that the address you provide for yourself is where you actually live. If you want to try to hide your identity by opening an account in the name of offshore trusts with puppet trustees who own corporations in other jurisdictions, you may as well quit now. That's not to say that offshore trusts are off limits; quite the contrary! Many of our clients at Profile Investment Services, Ltd. operate their finances through legal structures rather than directly in their own name, and that's fine. The problem arises when a someone tries to hide who he really is.

3. Clearly identify your citizenship. One common mistake that people make when opening an account is not understanding whether they must sign a W-8 or W-9 form. These forms tell the brokerage firm whether you're opening the account as a U.S. citizen or as a non-U.S. citizen. If you have U.S. citizenship but live in another country, you still must sign a W-9.

4. Understand what benefits you are getting. An important distinction to understand is that when you open an account, you are generally signing up for two distinct services: (a) Advice, (b) Custody/clearing. The advice should normally come from someone who is licensed both in and outside the United States. Understanding the special needs and tax considerations of U.S. citizens who live beyond the American borders is the purview of an elite type of cross-border specialist. Don't just count on your old accountant or financial advisor to comprehend the nuances of an overseas lifestyle. The custody and clearing should come from a major brokerage firm so that you get a full range of services. Those include, first and foremost, insuring your account. The most common type of insurance would be through the SIPC (Securities Investor Protection Corpo-

ration), and then normally third-party insurance above and beyond that. Other services would include:

- access to world markets,

- currency trading,

- a selection of funds and money managers, and

- easy access to your money through a Visa/ MasterCard and checkbook.

5. Pose these four questions. Along with the "standard" queries you might want to make when selecting an advisor, be sure to ask:

   - What experience do you have in dealing with cross-border clients?

   - Do you provide cross-border financial planning as well as investment services?

   - Can you set me up with an actual brokerage account, or do I have to do that on my own?

   - Will the brokerage account be in my own name, or are my assets combined with other people's?

6. Meet the advisor. Depending on your locale, you may or may not meet with the advisor. At

Profile, though I prefer to meet all of my new clients, I understand it's not always possible. In those cases, I set up phone meetings or Skype calls in which I'll spend all the time needed to get to know the client as we are getting started. Though there's nothing like a face-to-face meeting, a video conference is a pretty good substitute.

7. Sign the paperwork and fund the account. Signing paperwork normally doesn't take much time, except if you have to mail forms back and forth. Once that's completed, the advisor should open your account and then it's up to you to fund it. The best way to fund the account is to wire money from your current account in your name to the new account, which is also in your name. Compliance officers who oversee money transfers always prefer to see money moving to and from "same name" accounts. Never try to fund accounts with cash or travelers' checks since those are often signs of money laundering. Also, don't plan to deposit funds into the account and then send the money out immediately. That's also an indication that the account is not really meant for investment purposes, and the company's compliance team will begin investigating

it. If they suspect any sort of foul play, they have the right to freeze the account.

8. Tell the advisor if you have any special needs or requests. Though I've noted a number of situations where compliance officers may flag an account as a potential problem, that doesn't mean that people don't have special situations sometimes. If you're involved in a business deal or if you're getting divorced, for example, you might have certain requirements in handling your money. Make sure you bring those issues up before opening the account and ask the advisor to check with his legal team to make sure that everyone is on the same page. The best way to insure smooth operation of your account is to have open and honest communication from the outset.

9. How to choose the right investments. At this point, you've interviewed the advisor, opened the account, and funded it, too. What's next? Explain your goals to your advisor, as well as your risk tolerance. Hopefully he will ask you a lot of questions to help you develop an investment strategy that makes sense for your situation. If you feel pressured to make a particular purchase, then beware of the advisor. Investment

professionals should spend their time educating you about your choices, not pushing you to invest in something.

10. Monitor the account. Using the online account lookup service that the brokerage firm should provide, keep a close eye on your holdings. Even though you may not trade regularly, it's good financial hygiene to keep track of what's going on with your money. Ultimately, you are the one responsible for your funds, so be sure to watch your account at least once a month. On the flip side, make sure not to fall into the other extreme of watching your account too much – like on an hourly basis. For most long-term investors, this close monitoring is not useful, will add stress, and will often lead to too much trading.

For over twenty years, I've been helping people who live outside of the United States open U.S. brokerage accounts. In the past few years, I've watched how the regulatory environment has made it more difficult for some companies to handle cross-border clients. However, I've also found that there are so many opportunities for folks who have U.S. brokerage accounts to invest in such a wide variety of securities, that I think it's critical for many people to handle their investments through a U.S. brokerage account.

To see a free, short video called, "U.S. Brokerage Accounts for Non-U.S. Residents," go to our free resource page at:

www.Profile-Financial.com/inheritancebook.

If you have any specific questions or would like some help getting set up with your own U.S. brokerage account or retirement account (IRA), feel free to contact me at **www.Profile-Financial.com.**

Douglas Goldstein, CFP® is the author of the best-selling books *The Expatriate's Guide to Handling Money and Taxes, Building Wealth in Israel,* and *Rich As A King: How the Wisdom of Chess Can Make You a Grandmaster of Investing*, which he wrote with World Chess Champion Susan Polgar. (Visit www.RichAsAKing.com to sign up for the *Rich As A King* blog with strategic investing tips.) Securities offered through Portfolio Resources Group, Inc. Member FINRA, SIPC, MSRB, FSI. Call (02) 624-2788 for a consultation about handling your U.S. investments from Israel. The opinions expressed are those of the author and not necessarily those of Portfolio Resources Group, Inc. or its affiliates.

Appendix C

What to Do Immediately When Someone Passes Away

When a family member dies, people often find themselves in a fog, unable to prioritize, organize, or even keep track of what's going on. This short checklist provides a list of some of the most common tasks and responsibilities that next-of-kin most often handle immediately after a death. Though every family will have its own concerns, use the following as a starting point as you deal with a loss.

• Keep track of everything. Whether you send a letter to an insurance company, pay for taxis to bring relatives to the funeral, or even just have a conversation with a distant cousin, write it down. You will likely forget anything that you haven't recorded. Many expenditures that you make now may be reimbursed by the deceased's estate, so make a note of what you spent, and ideally keep the receipt. Technically oriented people might like to use a program like Evernote, Microsoft OneNote, or Apple Notes, which will allow you to set up sub-notebooks, add photographs and scans to your records, and even make audio recordings. These programs synchronize with the cloud so you can access and update the information all the time on your phone, tablet, or computer. Of course, a good old-fashioned notebook would work, too.

- Determine if the person wanted to donate organs. Many people in Israel sign up to become donors by getting an "Adi card" (named after Ehud Ben Dror, who died while waiting for a kidney donation). To sign up as an organ donor in Israel, go to adi.gov.il/en.

- Contact the burial society, *"chevra kadisha."* In Israel, all people are entitled to a free burial in the cemetery of the town where they lived. Some people choose to buy burial plots if they have a specific place that they want to be buried. See if there is any record that the deceased may have made some alternative arrangements.

- Arrange for care for any dependents, including pets.

- Check the insurance policies.

  - After a person dies, his auto insurance may no longer allow for other drivers to be covered. The executor of the estate may be covered, but double check with the insurance agent *before* you take the car out for a spin since you may not be insured.

  - Home insurance policies will remain in force if the deceased kept up paying the bills. But sometimes people towards the end of their lives lose track of some of their obligations and may have let the insurance lapse. If the house is no longer insured, work on this right away. It could take a long time between a person passing and the sale of the property, at which point responsibility passes to the new owners. In the meantime, if someone gets hurt on the property or if there's damage to the house, the assets of the estate could be fully liable.

  - Health insurance can probably be canceled, but confirm that no other family members are connected to the policy so that they don't lose their protection.

- Maintain physical upkeep and protection of property.

  ○ Confirm the car is parked in a secure and legal area.

  ○ Have someone keep an eye on the home.

  ○ Check phone messages and the mail.

  ○ Throw out perishable food and water plants.

  ○ Tell the local police the house is empty and ask them to keep an eye on it.

- Pay important bills promptly. Even after people die, their bills keep coming. Continue paying the critical ones like the mortgage and credit card bills. Consider canceling others, such as the cable TV and internet, if they won't be needed in the house anymore.

- As you prepare to sell the home, make sure there are no outstanding obligations or debts related to it. For example, if the deceased had been planning to sell the house and signed with a real estate agent, the executor may be obligated to use that agent until the contract expires.

- Ask for at least 10 original death certificates, as many banks, brokerage firms, credit bureaus, and companies may each require one. Since many firms will refuse a photocopy, request a lot of certified originals when taken care of by the hospital, burial society, or funeral home.

• Contact credit bureaus and tell them about the death to avoid identity theft. When these agencies receive copies of the death certificate, they mark the files of the deceased so that no credit cards can be issued in their names. Check out the requirements at the websites of the three major American credit agencies: www.experian.com, www.transunion.com, www.equifax.com.

www.ingramcontent.com/pod-product-compliance
Lightning Source LLC
Chambersburg PA
CBHW020208200326

41521CB00005BA/291